D1327484

Being Black

NEW BEACON BOOKS ⬤NB⬤ LONDON. PORT OF SPAIN

By Roxy Harris

First published in 1981 by New Beacon Books Ltd., 76 Stroud
Green Road, London N4 3EN

© 1970 *Soledad Brother* (extracts) World Entertainers Ltd
© 1968 *Soul on Ice* (extracts) Eldridge Cleaver
© 1981 text Roxy Harris

All rights reserved. No part of this book may be reproduced in
any form or by any means without prior written permission of
the publisher, excepting brief quotes used in connection with
reviews written specifically for inclusion in a magazine or
newspaper.

ISBN 0 901241 39 3

Photo credits:
Camera Press: p.7 (Pickets outside court); p.9; p.11; p.26; p.30;
    p.32; p.35; p.37; p.39; p.45; p.51.
Elizabeth Wilson: p.17; p.19; p.24.
Bob Scott: p.31.
Keystone: p.48.

Cover and Book designed by Julian Stapleton

Burgess
E
185.625
.H37
1981g
c.2

Printed by Villiers Publications Ltd., Ingestre Rd., London NW5

A Note on the Use of the Book:—

This book is intended to be used by readers in one of three ways. Readers could:—
1. Use it with a teacher or friend.
2. Use it with a group of friends.
3. Use it on their own.

Here also are some suggestions as to how the reader could approach each selection in the book:—

1. *When used with a teacher:*—

(i) Read the selection and questions — ask if there is anything you do not understand.

(ii) Write down your answers to the questions.

(iii) Let the teacher read your answers and challenge you to defend what you have written.

(iv) Ask the teacher to point out any badly written sentences and spelling mistakes in your answers.

2. *When used with a group of friends:*—

(i) One member of the group reads the selection and questions out aloud while the others follow from their own copies of the book.

(ii) Each member of the group should say what answer he/she would give to each question. Discussion should then follow. Each member of the group can either agree with or challenge the opinions expressed by the others in the group.

3. *When used on your own:*—

(i) Read the selections and questions.

(ii) Write down your answers (writing them down will help you to clarify your thoughts).

(iii) Consult other books to get more information about the people mentioned in the Notes.

Roxy Harris

The idea of using selections from *Soledad Brothers* and *Soul on Ice*, in this way, came out of work with black youth in schools. These young black school students showed a strong desire for reading material with which they could make some connection, and which would enable them to explore their own experience. They wanted to assert their distinctiveness as young blacks, but faced secondary school courses which focussed exclusively on the white, European experience of the world. The school curriculum rejected or, at best, avoided the suggestion that blacks, because of their own particular historical experience, have a valid view of the world which is different from that normally accepted by most whites.

The extracts in this collection were deliberately made short, so that the contents of *Soledad Brother* and *Soul on Ice* would be more accessible to many readers who might not feel able to tackle the books as a whole. The questions accompanying the selections were framed in an open-ended way so that they could be answered by people at different levels. Nevertheless, there was a deeper motivation behind the inclusion of the questions. They were intended to give black readers an opportunity for self-definition.

In Britain, blacks have been generally absent from the main-stream newspapers, as well as from TV and radio programmes. As a consequence they have grown accustomed to being swamped by white commentators' interpretations and definitions of the black political, economic, social and cultural experience. An important part of a man's independence and freedom depends on his ability to define himself for himself, and to choose the directions he wishes to take, instead of having his frames of reference defined by someone else.

Soledad Brother and *Soul on Ice* are particularly relevant to the British situation in that they highlight many of the issues confronting blacks when they are a minority in a white, advanced urban society.

For example, how should blacks react when the media parade a "successful" black to prove that black anger against the system is unjustified?

Why are whites willing to allow blacks to "make it" in the fields of entertainment and sport, but are hostile to the idea of black access to other areas?

I hope that consideration of these questions and others raised in this collection will help black people, young and not so young, to sort out for themselves where they stand on many of the crucial political, social, economic and cultural issues that they face.

London 1980   Roxy Harris

Soledad Brother Selections are taken from Penguin Books, 1971 edition.
Soul on Ice Selections from Panther Modern Society, 1970 edition.
Page references are given at the end of each excerpt.

George Jackson

GEORGE JACKSON

George Jackson was born in 1942 into a poor black family. He grew up in Chicago and in Los Angeles. In his teens he had many brushes with the police. Finally, when he was 18, he was accused of helping to rob a petrol station of 70 dollars and was jailed. His lawyer had told him that if he pleaded guilty he would get a light sentence. Instead, when he pleaded guilty, he got a heavy sentence of one year to life and lost his right to appeal. In the United States the sentence of "one year to life" means that a prisoner can have his case considered once a year by a Parole Board. The Board can release him if, in its opinion, his record in prison is satisfactory. This system inflicts a kind of mental torture on prisoners such as George. They spend each year before the Parole Board meets hoping against hope that they will be released: and year after year the Board turns them down. Each year prison guards tried to provoke George into "spoiling" his record so that he would be refused parole.

From 1960 until his death in 1971 George Jackson spent most of his time in San Quentin and Soledad, prisons full of violence between black and white prisoners, and white guards and black prisoners. In early 1970, three black prisoners were shot dead in Soledad prison by a prison guard. Soon afterwards a white prison guard was killed in revenge. George Jackson and two others, who came to be known as The Soledad Brothers, were charged with killing the guard. Later in 1970 George's brother Jonathan Jackson was shot dead after a raid on a court house, in an effort to free his brother whom he thought would get no justice from the courts. Angela Davis, George's close friend, was arrested in October 1970, on a charge of providing the guns for Jonathan's raid. George Jackson felt sure that he would not be allowed to leave prison alive. He was certain that the prison authorities tried to provoke him so that they would have an excuse for killing him.

On August 21, 1971, George Jackson was murdered at San Quentin prison. The authorities claim that Jackson was shot dead while trying to escape. However, it is now clear that the prison authorities conspired to murder him. In April, 1972, the surviving Soledad Brothers were found not guilty of all charges against them.

George Jackson spent 11 years in prison, much of it in isolation, and was killed there, all for allegedly helping to steal 70 dol-

Angela Davis on trial

Pickets outside the court

lars. The person who actually took the money was released after three years.

These extracts from *Soledad Brother* were letters he wrote to family and friends.

Selection 1

When blacks are a minority in a white society, they must not rely on the parliament or law courts of that society to give them justice. Blacks must liberate themselves. Blacks must rely on themselves to fight for what they want.

When this book comes out, the man who wrote it will still be in his Soledad[1] cell, with his Soledad Brothers.* What follows must be read as a manifesto, as a tract, as a call to rebellion, since it is that first of all.

5 It is too obvious that the legislative and judiciary systems of the United States were established in order to protect a capitalist minority and, if forced, the whole of the white population; but these infernal systems are still raised against the black man. We have known for a long time now that the
10 black man is, from the start, natively, the guilty man. We can be sure that if the blacks, by the use of their violence, their intelligence, their poetry, all that they have accumulated for centuries while observing their former masters in silence and in secrecy – if the blacks do not undertake their own
15 liberation, the whites will not make a move.

But already Huey Newton,[2] Bobby Seale,[3] the members of the Black Panther[4] party, George Jackson, and others have stopped lamenting their fate. The time for blues is over, for them. They are creating, each according to his means, a
20 revolutionary consciousness. And their eyes are clear. Not blue.

Jean Genet[5]

*In late June 1970, before the publication of this book, the Soledad Brothers were transferred to San Quentin.[6]   (p.24)

8

Questions:
1. Do you think that black people should take action to improve their conditions or is it up to white people to start treating blacks better?
2. Some people say that blacks complain too much instead of doing more to help themselves. What is your opinion?

Words:
Manifesto (line 3) – a public statement of opinions
Tract (line 3) – a short booklet or pamphlet on politics
Legislative (line 5) – law making
Judiciary (line 5) – judges and courts
Accumulated (line 12) – built up
Liberation (line 15) – freedom or release
Lamenting (line 18) – weeping and wailing

Notes:
1. *Soledad* A men's prison in California, containing a hardline special punishment unit for prisoners that the authorities consider difficult.
2. *Huey Newton* One of the founder members of the Black Panther Party. Born in the State of Louisiana in 1942, he grew up in Oakland, California. In his teens he became involved with petty crime and street gangs and served a few short jail terms. In 1966, after being involved in several black organisations, he and Bobby Seale founded the Black Panther Party for Self Defence. Newton was admired in the black community for his bravery in facing up to the armed, racist police of Oakland. Also for his ability to challenge these police on points of law. In 1967 Huey Newton was accused of killing a policeman. He was kept in jail for a year before being convicted of manslaughter. He spent a further two years in jail before another court freed him on bail in August 1970. In 1971 he had to go through a second and third trial on the same charges, but the juries could not agree. Finally at the end of 1971 the trial judge was forced to dismiss all charges against him. In 1974 he was again accused of murder and when his life was constantly threatened he escaped to Cuba where he lived for 3 years. In 1977, feeling that the atmosphere in America had calmed down, he returned to America to face the charges against him. He got a hero's

Huey Newton after release from prison 1970

9

welcome in Oakland. In 1978 he was still engaged in a tough legal battle to have the charges dropped.

Bobby Seale

3. *Bobby Seale* Born in Dallas, Texas, in 1936. Founded the Black Panther Party along with Huey Newton in 1966. Valuable to the Panthers because of his organizing and speaking ability. In 1969 he was accused of murder, but it was 1971 before he was brought to trial. Seale challenged the right of white racist jurors to try him. Over 1000 people were questioned before an acceptable jury was found. Finally, in May 1971, the charges against him were dismissed. Meanwhile in March 1969, Seale and seven others, known together as the Chicago Eight, were charged with "crossing state lines to incite riots". During the trial there were many clashes between Bobby Seale and the Judge Hoffman. Hoffman had Seale gagged and chained to his chair after Seale had constantly accused him of being a racist and a fascist. Hoffman sentenced him to 4 years in jail for contempt of court and ordered a retrial. In September 1972, the Government had the charges against Bobby Seale dismissed. In 1973 Bobby Seale ran for election as Mayor of Oakland. He lost the election and since then little has been heard of him, although he is believed to be still working politically in the black community.

4. *Black Panther Party* Founded by Bobby Seale and Huey Newton in 1966 in Oakland, California. In the beginning the Panthers provided armed patrols to follow the police and step in when the police behaved improperly. The party also developed a ten-point programme for Black Liberation, and by 1969 had thousands of members all over the United States. However, the work of the Black Panthers was disrupted between 1968 and 1972, through the constant killing of its members and legal charges brought against those who escaped death. It has now become clear that the F.B.I., through its leader J. Edgar Hoover, mounted a campaign to smash the Panthers by any means possible.

In 1967 the F.B.I. developed a Counter-Intelligence Programme (Cointelpro) against the Black Panthers. Its aims included stopping different black groups getting together, getting rid of powerful black community leaders, stopping the Panthers from recruiting black youth, and stopping black groups such as the Panthers and its leaders from gaining

Black Panthers
drilling in California

respectability. Among its methods were the murder of many Panther members, and the incitement of others to murder Panthers; constant harassment of Panthers, sending fake letters to Panther leaders warning them of plots against them by fellow Panthers.

These and other methods defused the threat posed by the Black Panthers to white racism in the United States. Nevertheless, the Panthers have survived and are still active politically. More importantly, their example has inspired a whole generation of blacks all around the world.

5. *Jean Genet* Frenchman. Born in Paris 1900. Grew up in an orphanage. Lived in many European countries. Involved in crime. Constant jail sentences. Eventually became a famous writer.

6. *San Quentin* A men's prison in California. Like Soledad it is tough and brutal.

11

Selection 2

A black child may find the first white child he meets to be strange.

Seeing the white boys up close in kindergarten was a traumatic event. I *must* have seen some before in magazines or books but never in the flesh. I approached one, felt his hair, scratched at his cheek, he hit me in the head with a baseball
5 bat. They found me crumpled in a heap just outside the school-yard fence. (p.29)

Question:
1. Try to describe any times when you have been scared of white people.

Words:
Kindergarten (line 1) – infant school
Traumatic (line 1) – shocking

Selection 3

A black working man has to be aggressive to keep his dignity. This does not mean that he should fight against other black working-class people.

My grandfather, George 'Papa' Davis, stands out of those early years more than any other figure in my total environment. He was separated from his wife by the system. Work for men was impossible to find in Harrisburg. He was living
5 and working in Chicago — sending his wage back to the people downstate. He was an extremely aggressive man, and since aggression on the part of the slave means crime, he was in jail now and then. I loved him. He tried to direct my great energy into the proper form of protest. He invented long
10 simple allegories that always pictured the white politicians as animals (jackasses, toads, goats, vermin in general). He scorned the police with special enmity. He and my mother went to great pains to impress on me that it was the worst form of niggerism to hook and jab, cut and stab at other
15 blacks. (p. 33)

Questions:

1. What is your opinion of black people who commit crimes against other black people?
2. Write about any white people you know who try to make sure that black people are treated properly.

Words:

Environment (line 2) – surroundings
Aggressive (line 6) – angry, violently hostile to his enemies
Allegories (line 10) – stories which make their point in a round-about way
Scorned (line 12) – rejected

Selection 4

Prison is no joke. It is a hard, degrading experience with the prison authorities holding all the cards.

The very first time it was like dying. Just to exist at all in the cage calls for some heavy psychic readjustments. Being captured was the first of my fears. It may have been inborn. It may have been an acquired characteristic built up over the
5   centuries of black bondage. It is the thing I've been running from all my life. When it caught up to me in 1957 I was fifteen years old and not very well-equipped to deal with sudden changes. The Youth Authority joints are places that demand complete capitulation; one must cease to resist
10 altogether or else . . .
The employees are the same general types found lounging at all prison facilities. They need a job — any job; the state needs goons. Chino[1] was almost new at the time. The regular housing units were arranged so that at all times one could
15 see the lockup unit. I think they called it 'X'. We existed from day to day to avoid it. How much we ate was strictly controlled, so was the amount of rest. After lights went out, no one could move from his bed without a flash of the pigs' handlight. During the day the bed couldn't be touched.
20 There were so many compulsories that very few of us could manage to stay out of trouble even with our best efforts. Everything was programmed right down to the precise

George Jackson

spoonful. We were made to march in military fashion everywhere we went — to the gym, to the mess hall, to compul-
25 sory prayer meetings. And then we just marched. I pretended
that I couldn't hear well or understand anything but the
simplest directions so I was never given anything but the
simplest work. I was lucky; always when my mind failed me
I've had great luck to carry me through.
30   All my life I've done exactly what I wanted to do just when
I wanted, no more, perhaps less sometimes, but never any
more, which explains why I had to be jailed. 'Man was born
free. But everywhere he is in chains'. I never adjusted. I
haven't adjusted even yet, with half my life already spent in
35 prison. I can't truthfully say prison is any less painful now
than during that first experience.   (pp. 36-37)

Questions:
1. Why was George so frightened of being captured?
2. What do you think would happen to anyone who kept on
resisting?
3. Why were the prisoners forced to march about everywhere?

Word:
Capitulation (line 9) – surrender

Note:
1. *Chino* A men's prison in California. Not as tough as Soledad
or San Quentin.

Selection 5

*A person in prison or detention needs a plan to help him survive.
Reading assists this survival by keeping the mind active.*

Capture, imprisonment, is the closest to being dead that
one is likely to experience in this life. There were no beatings
(for me at least) in this youth joint and the food wasn't too
bad. I came through it. When told to do something I simply
5 played the idiot, and spent my time reading. The absentminded bookworm, I was in full revolt by the time seven
months were up.   (p. 38)

14

Question:
1. Some prisoners spend most of their time in prison fighting the guards others just read books. What would you do with your time if you were in jail?

Words:
Absentminded (line 5) – forgetful
Bookworm (line 6) – a person who spends a large part of his/her time reading books

---
Selection 6

Many whites do not value any black person highly. Blacks can turn this white weakness to their own advantage.

    When they called him to be released that morning, I went out in his place. I've learned one very significant thing for our struggle here in the U.S.: all blacks do look alike to certain types of white people. White people tend to grossly under-
5   estimate all blacks, out of habit. Blacks have been over-estimating whites in a conditioned reflex.   (p. 39)

Questions:
1. How true is it that some people think that all blacks look alike?
2. Say if you agree or disagree that whites think that black people will be useless at doing things.

Words:
Grossly (line 4) – completely or totally
Underestimate (line 4) – to make out that something is inferior to what it really is
Conditioned Reflex (line 6) – automatic reaction

Older blacks are often willing to accept a worse position in white society than younger blacks.

I guess you are right in what you say about Mother's position. If she wishes to occupy the corner set aside for us in this society and be happy with such then let it be. I merely speak of better and different things in a society
5 greater (in my humble opinion) and more conducive to advancement for people of my kind. Always bear in mind that though I may sound intolerant and pressing at times, all I say is by way of discourse and nothing by way of advance. You see I understand you people clearly. You are afflicted by
10 the same set of principles that has always governed black people's ideas and habits here in the U.S. I know also how we arrived at this appalling state of decadence. You see, my father, we have been 'educated' into an acceptance of our positions as national scapegraces. Our acceptance of the lie
15 is consciously based on the supposition that peace can and must be preserved at any price. Blacks here in the U.S. apparently do not care how well they live, but are only concerned with how long they are able to live. This is odd indeed when considering that it is possible for us to live well, but
20 within the reach of no man to live long! My deepest and most sincerely felt sympathies go out to all of you who are not able to resolve your problems because of this fundamental lack of spirit. The morass of illusionment has claimed your souls completely. (pp. 57-58)

Questions:
1. Some people say that blacks in Britain should accept their poor position and not make too much fuss. What do you think?
2. Black people are often blamed when things go wrong in Britain. Try to give some examples.

Words:
Conducive (line 5) – likely to produce, likely to lead to
Intolerant (line 7) – hostile towards other people's views
Discourse (line 8) – talk, conversation
Afflicted by (line 9) – suffering from
Decadence (line 12) – rottenness
Supposition (line 15) – opinion

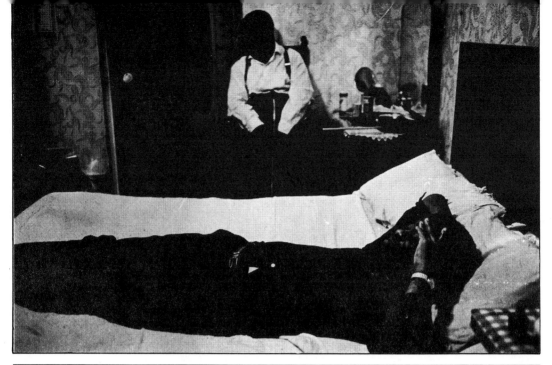

Selection 8

Black parents should do more than simply attack their teenage children for doing wrong. They should guide their children as to who their enemies in society are. They should also advise their children about how to get things they want without getting into trouble.

I would not be in prison now if she hadn't been reading
life through those rose-coloured glasses of hers, or if you
would have had time and the wisdom to tell me of my
enemies, and how to get the things I needed without falling
5 into their traps. She kept telling me how wrong I was and
making me feel guilty. All of this I now understand, but
again cannot forgive because she is still doing this same sort
of thing!!   (p. 59)

Questions:
1. Try to describe times when your parents have told you off for getting into trouble at school or in the street, but have not told you how you are supposed to avoid trouble.
2. What would you do if you had no money to buy some records or clothes which your friends all had?

Blacks in white societies have been allowed recognition only in a few limited activities.

I'm glad you weren't a singer or dancer. Pop was wise in that. The image held of the blacks in this part of the world is that we are proficient in but one or two areas only, the service trades or the physical entertainment fields (singers,
5 dancers, boxers, baseball players).

Would you like to support the theory that we are good for nothing but to serve or entertain our captors?   (p. 64)

Questions:
1. Is it true that black people are naturally better at singing, dancing and sport than other people? If so, why?
2. Why is George so glad that his mother wasn't a singer or dancer?

Word:
Proficient (line 3) – skilled

Selection 10

Each individual black blames himself for failing in life. This is wrong. The truth is that blacks in a white society have little or no control over their own lives, but they must get this control.

You must realize, understand fully, that we have little or no control over our lives. You must then stop giving yourself pain by feeling that you failed somewhere. You have not failed. You have been failed, by history and events, and
5 people over whom you had no control. Only after you understand this can you then go on to make the necessary alterations that will bring some purpose and value to your life; you must gain some control! I have said this to Robert[1] a hundred times but it makes no impression at all. He writes
10 back in the same vein as he did the time before I said anything. He just doesn't have the mental equipment. Will you look deeper and think on the matter and then explain to

him? I was born knowing exactly nothing. I had no one, no one, to teach me the things of real value. The school systems are gauged to teach youth what to think, not how to think. Robert[1] never had the time to say even hello, and neither of you really knew anything to give me anyway, because your parents knew nothing. Do you see where the cycle brings us, to the real source of the trouble, the alienation and the abandonment, the pressure from without, the system and its supporters? I didn't know either. So we must look to the people whose responsibility it is to see to it that the benefits of society pass down to all concerned for an answer. If a good god exists then they are the ones who must make an appeal to him for forgiveness: forgiveness for relinquishment and dereliction of duty! I don't need god, religion, belief, etc. I need control, control of the determining factors relating to the unquestioning support and loyalty of my mother, father, brothers, sisters. (pp. 67-68)

Questions:
1. George says that " . . . we have little or no control over our lives." Do you agree with this?
2. George writes "I don't need god, religion, belief etc". Is religion any use to someone in trouble?

Words:
Gauged (line 15) – designed or set exactly
Alienation (line 19) – feeling of *not* being part of something or *not* belonging somewhere

Note:
1. *Robert* George Jackson's father.

Black people react differently to the pressures on them. Some give in to the pressure. Others rebel, but in a confused fashion.

Dear Father,

I haven't read anything or studied in a week now. I have been devoting all my time to thought. I trust you are all in health. I think of my personal past quite often. This is un-
5 comfortable sometimes but necessary. I try not to let my past mistakes bother me too much, though some seem almost unpardonable. If it were not for the few intermixed little victories, my confidence in my ability would be irreparably shaken.

10 Though I know I am a victim of social injustice and economic pressure and though I understand the forces that work to drive so many of our kind to places like this and to mental institutions, I can't help but know that I proceeded wrong somewhere. I could have done a lot worse. You know
15 our people react in different ways to this neoslavery, some just give in completely and join the other side. They join some christian cult and cry out for integration. These are the ones who doubt themselves most. They are the weakest and hardest to reach with the new doctrine. Some become in-
20 veterate drinkers and narcotic users in an attempt to gain some mental solace for the physical depravity they suffer. I've heard them say, 'There's no hope without dope'. Some hire on as a janitor, bellboy, redcap, cook, elevator boy, singer, boxer, baseball player, or maybe a freak at some sideshow
25 and pretend that all is as well as is possible. They think since it's always been this way it must always remain this way; these are the fatalists, they serve and entertain and rationalize.

Then there are those who resist and rebel but do not know
30 what, who, why, or how exactly they should go about this. They are aware but confused. They are the least fortunate, for they end where I have ended. By using half measures and failing dismally to effect any real improvement in their con-dition, they fall victim to the full fury and might of the
35 system's repressive agencies. (pp. 70-71)

Questions:
1. Why do some black people "join some Christian cult" or become "drinkers and narcotics users"?
2. What happens to black people who "resist and rebel" in a confused way, without a clear head?

Words:
Cult (line 17) – unusual religion, fake religion

Inveterate (line 19) – firmly established, addicted

Solace (line 21) – comfort

Rationalize (line 28) – try to give a reasonable explanation for events

Repressive (line 35) – controlling by force

It is not enough for blacks to chase after a college education. Blacks can only advance their position when they find out the truth about their history and way of life.

It is difficult, very difficult to get any facts concerning our history and our way of life. The lies, half-truths, and propaganda have won total sway over the facts. We have no knowledge of our heritage. Our economic status has reduced
5 our minds to a state of complete oblivion. The young black who comes out of college or the university is as ignorant and unlearned as the white labourer. For all practical purposes he is worse off than when he went in, for he has learned only the attitudes and ways of the snake, and a few well-worded
10 lies. The ruling culture refuses to let us know how much we did to advance civilization in our lands long ago.   (p. 76)

Questions:
1. Why do you think it is so difficult to get facts about the history and way of life of black people?
2. What does Jackson mean when he says that a young black at college or university "has learned only the attitudes and ways of the snake"?

Words:
Propaganda (line 2) – one-sided information or misleading information
Heritage (line 4) – information and way of life passed on to us by our forefathers
Oblivion (line 5) – forgetfulness
Culture (line 10) – kind of civilization

Selection 13

The jails in the United States are full of blacks who turned to crime to lift themselves from the bottom level of society.

I know that few blacks over here have ever been free. The forms of slavery merely *changed* at the signing of the Emancipation Proclamation[1] from chattel slavery to economic

slavery. If you could see and talk to some of the blacks I meet
5 in here you would immediately understand what I mean, and
see that I'm right. They are all average, all with the same
backgrounds, and in for the same thing, some form of food
getting. About 70 to 80 per cent of all crime in the U.S. is
perpetrated by blacks, 'the sole reason for this is that 98 per
10 cent of our number live below the poverty level in bitter and
abject misery'! You must take off your rose-coloured glasses
and stop pretending.   (pp. 81-82)

Question:
1. Do you think that the reason why so many black people commit crimes is because they are poor? Or is there some other
reason?

Words:
Emancipation (line 3) – freedom
Proclamation (line 3) – announcement
Chattel (line 3) – personal property that the owner can move
around as he wishes
Perpetrated (line 9) – carried out, committed
Abject (line 11) – despairing

Note:
1. *Emancipation Proclamation* The statement made on January
1st 1863 by the American President Abraham Lincoln, which
announced that slaves were to be freed.

Selection 14

Black women have stood up to the strains and shocks of black history, far better than black men.

You are right of course in what you contend. The black woman has in the past few hundred years been the only force holding us together and holding us up. She has absorbed the biggest part of the many shocks and strains of existence
5   under a slave order. The men can think of nothing more effective than pimping, gambling, or petty theft. I've heard men brag about being pimps of black women and taking money from black women who are on relief. Things like this I find odious, disgusting — you are right, the black men have
10   proven themselves to be utterly detestable and repulsive in the past. Before I would succumb to such subterfuge I would scratch my living from the ground on hands and knees, or die in a hail of bullets! My hat goes off to every one of you, you have my profoundest respect. I have surrendered all hope

of happiness for myself in this life to the prospect of
effecting some improvement in our circumstances as a whole.
I have a plan, I will give, and give, and give myself until it
proves our making or my end. The men of our group have
developed as a result of living under a ruthless system a set
of mannerisms that numb the soul. We have been made the
floor mat of the world, but the world has yet to see what can
be done by men of our nature, by men who have walked the
path of disparity, of regression, of abortion, and yet come
out whole. There will be a special page in the book of life
for the men who have crawled back from the grave. This page
will tell of utter defeat, ruin, passivity, and subjection in
one breath, and in the next, overwhelming victory and ful-
filment.

So take care of yourself, and hold on. (pp. 94-95)

Questions:
1. Why does George think that "black men have proven themselves to be utterly detestable and repulsive in the past"?
2. What does Jackson mean when he says that black men "have
been made the floor mat of the world"?
3. Why is he so proud of black women?

Words:
Odious (line 9) — disgusting, repulsive
Succumb (line 11) — give in
Subterfuge (line 11) — attempt to escape from reality
Passivity (line 26) — lack of action
Subjection (line 26) — complete obedience

Selection 15

---

*So many white people seem to have a desire to dominate every-
thing with which they come into contact. This attitude is hard to
understand.*

But I do sometimes wonder just exactly how they got the
way they are. I know beyond question the extent of the evil
that lurks in their hearts; I see the *insane* passion, inherent in
their characters, to dominate all that they come in contact

5   with. What aggressive psychosis impels a man to want his
    dessert and mine too, to want to feast at every table, to
    want to cast his shadow over every land? I don't know what
    they are; some folks call them devils (doers of evil). I don't
    know if this is an adequate description. It goes much
10 deeper.   (p. 109)

Questions:

1. Jackson wonders why so many white men have had the wish to
   rule over other people's countries and control their lives. Why
   do you think they have done this?
2. Give some examples of countries which English people have
   ruled over.

Words:

Inherent (line 3) – an essential part
Dominate (line 4) – control
Aggressive (line 5) – violent
Psychosis (line 5) – serious mental illness, a kind of madness
Impels (line 5) – drives forward

Selection 16

Beating a child does not teach him to behave correctly.

There are three ways to enforce and build discipline in a child: through terror, through guilt, and through shame. The first principle is the worst and involves keeping the child in constant fear of beating or harsh reprimand. This is not
5 conducive to all-round adjustment. Either the child becomes a confirmed coward or at best unstable and erratic. A child with feelings of insecurity (lack of confidence) may later on try to prove himself by deliberately doing things against what he has been taught is right. Think on that a moment!

(p. 127)

Questions:
1. What effect do beatings have on a child?
2. Give examples of times when you or your friends have deliberately done things against what you have been taught is right.

Words:
Enforce (line 1) – put into effect
Reprimand (line 4) – criticism or telling off
Conducive (line 5) – likely to produce, likely to lead to
Erratic (line 6) – aimless

Selection 17

Black people will suffer great unhappiness as long as they try to imitate white culture instead of relying on their own culture and way of life.

Please don't take what I expressed in my last letter too seriously. I was feeling extremely bad. Try to relax; the mental depression you are presently gripped by comes from a very common cause, particularly among us blacks here in
5 the U.S. As a defence, we look at life through our rose-coloured glasses, rationalizing and pretending that things are not so bad after all, but then day after day — tragedy after tragedy strikes and confuses us, and our pretence fails

to aid or dispel the nagging feeling that we cannot have
10 security in an insecure society, especially when one belongs
to an insecure caste within this larger society. I believe
sincerely that you will be a very ·unhappy and perplexed
woman for as long as you try to pretend that you have anything in common with this culture, or better, that this
15 culture has anything in common with you, and as long as you
pretend that there is no difference between men, and as long
as you try to be more English than the English, while the
English ignore your attempts and use your humility to their
advantage. (pp. 113-114)

Questions:

1. What does it mean to look at life through "rose-coloured glasses"?
2. Why does George think that it is no use trying to be "more English than the English"?

Words:

Rationalizing (line 6) – trying to give a logical explanation
Dispel (line 9) – drive away
Caste (line 11) – an exclusive group of people in society who are exclusive for reasons such as their skin colour, race, or the family they are born into
Perplexed (line 12) – confused or puzzled
Culture (line 14) – kind of civilization
Humility (line 18) – humble attitude, modesty

Selection 18

Some blacks value only the flashy things in life.

I have experienced the same thing with women and men.
All the women I've had tried to use me, tried to secure
through me a soft spot in the cut-throat system for themselves. All they ever wanted was clothes and money and to
5 be taken out to flash these things. I no longer have time for
such small ideas or small people. Blacks that I've met here
who exhibit such characteristics I disdain and ignore. The
same with any woman I may have when I get out. She must
let me retrain her mind or no deal. (p. 118)

Questions:
1. How important do you think it is to have flashy clothes and plenty of money?
2. Why does Jackson have no time for people who think flashy clothes and money are important?

Words:
Exhibit (line 7) – show
Disdain (line 7) – look down on, despise

Selection 19

Control over your own life is more important than money or entertainment.

There can be no ties of blood or kinship strong enough to move me from my course, I'll never trade my self-determination for a car, cheap mass-produced clothes, clapboard house, or a couple of nights a week at the go-go. Control
5 over the circumstances that surround my existence is of the first importance to me.   (pp. 122-123)

Questions:
1. What do you think that "self-determination" means?
2. Why does Jackson refuse to trade his self-determination for a car, cheap mass-produced clothes, clapboard house, or a couple of nights a week at the go-go?

Word:
Kinship (line 1) – family relationship

Blacks should suspect any black who tries to encourage hatred against all whites. This is dangerous especially when blacks are a minority in white society. It also causes confusion when black police or soldiers appear in the front line against black demonstrations.

Who is the black working for, who does he love when he screams 'Honky'? He would throw us into a fight where we would be outnumbered 1 to 14 (counting the blacks who would fight with/for the other side in a race war). War on
5 the honky, it's just another mystification, if not an *outright* move by the fascist. *I don't know,* I don't pretend to clairvoyance, I can't read *all* thoughts, and I do know some whites that I wouldn't count as enemies, but if *all* whites were my enemies would it make sense for me to fight them
10 all at the same time? The blanket indictment of the white

Black police in Philadelphia

race has done nothing but perplex us, inhibit us. The theory
that all whites are the immediate enemy and all blacks our
brothers (making them loyal) is silly and indicative of a lazy
mind (to be generous, since it could be a fascist plot). It
15 doesn't explain the black pig; there were six on the Hampton-
Clark[1] kill. It doesn't explain the black paratroopers (just
more pigs) who put down the great Detroit[2] riot, and it
doesn't explain the pseudo-bourgeois who can be found
almost everywhere in the halls of government working for
20 white supremacy, fascism, and capitalism. It leaves the
average brother confused. In Detroit they just didn't know
what to do when they encountered the black paratroopers.
They were so stunned when they saw those black fools
shooting at them that they probably never will listen to
25 another black voice regardless of what it's saying.

(pp. 254-255)

Questions:

1. Black people are outnumbered in Britain. So how much good
   do you think it would do to try to defeat prejudiced white
   people just by using violence?
2. How true is it that only a stupid black person thinks that all
   blacks are our brothers and all whites our enemies?

Words:

Mystification (line 5) – something puzzling or confusing
Fascist (line 6) – person whose political beliefs are based on a
hatred of Communism and a hatred of other races. Such people
especially hate black people and Jews. Perhaps the best known
Fascists in history have been Hitler (Germany), Mussolini (Italy),
Franco (Spain)
Clairvoyance (line 6) – awareness of things that most human
beings cannot see, hear, touch, or smell
Indictment (line 10) – charge or accusation
Pseudo (line 18) – false or fake

Notes:

1. *Fred Hampton & Mark Clark* Two Black Panthers killed in
   suspicious circumstances by Chicago police in 1969.
2. *Detroit Riot* Black riot in Detroit in 1967 against racism and
   police violence. Part of the city was burnt down.

Eldridge Cleaver

ELDRIDGE CLEAVER

Eldridge Cleaver was born in Arkansas in 1935 and grew up in California. From the age of 15 until he was 30, he spent his time in and out of prison. This included a 14 year sentence for rape. While in prison he became first a Black Muslim then later a follower of Malcolm X. He wrote much of *Soul on Ice* in prison. He was released on parole in 1966 and in February 1967 joined the Black Panthers. Cleaver helped to edit and write the Black Panther newspaper.

In April 1968 Eldridge Cleaver and another Black Panther called Bobby Hutton were attacked by the police in Oakland, California. Hutton was shot dead and Cleaver wounded. This incident led, in the end, to Cleaver's parole being stopped. In autumn 1968, he was ordered back to jail. However, in November 1968 he escaped to Cuba by way of Canada. Cleaver and his wife, Kathleen, who was also a Black Panther, were invited to Algeria by the Algerian Government in July 1969 to attend the Pan-African Cultural Festival. They stayed, and, between 1970 and 1972, Cleaver acted as head of the Black Panther Party's International Section from Algiers. During 1971 Cleaver's differences with the Panthers became more and more serious and in that year he finally left the party. Late in 1972 he also quarrelled with the Algerian Government and was put under house arrest. He finally escaped to Paris in 1973, and returned to America in 1976/1977. Cleaver now says that after his experience of "socialist" countries such as Cuba, Algeria and North Vietnam, he has completely changed his view of America. He insists that it is a wonderful country in which he, as a black man, can get justice. Although he has tried to make his peace with the U.S. Government, he is still in trouble with the law. It seems that he now has a close interest in "born again" Christian movements.

It is not easy to find out exactly what went wrong between Eldridge Cleaver and the Black Panthers. However, it seems clear that after the publication of *Soul on Ice* in 1968, Cleaver enjoyed the excitement of his T.V. and radio appearances, and the flattery of young white radicals much more than the hard, patient work required by the Panthers. As the Black Panther leader Huey Newton put it: "He seemed to work with enthusiasm only after something sensational had taken place . . . He never taught one class or attempted to organize any programmes. He was always off talking on radio and television and before all sorts of groups that seemed more glamorous and exciting to him."[1] Speaking in 1977 the West Indian historian Walter Rodney said, " . . . revolutionary struggle is about consistency and about the capacity to sustain struggle and dedication, irrespective of the consequences. The record of Cleaver, not only with respect to Cuba, but before that, is one that leaves much to be desired."[2]

In spite of this, it is safe to say that in *Soul on Ice,* and elsewhere, Cleaver made a great contribution to Black Consciousness in the 1960's.

References:
1. *Revolutionary Suicide* by Huey P. Newton
2. 'Afras Review', No. 3.

Selection 1

Cleaver realizes that the image of white girls has a bigger place in his mind than that of black girls.

But I was genuinely beside myself with anger: almost every cell, excepting those of the homosexuals, had a pinup girl on the wall and the guards didn't bother them. Why, I asked the guard the next day, had he singled me out for special
5   treatment?

'Don't you know we have a rule against pasting up pictures on the walls?' he asked me.

'Later for the rules,' I said. 'You know as well as I do that that rule is not enforced.'
10   'Tell you what,' he said, smiling at me (the smile put me on my guard), 'I'll compromise with you: get yourself a coloured girl for a pinup — no white women — and I'll let it stay up. Is that a deal?'

I was more embarrassed than shocked. He was laughing in
15   my face. I called him two or three dirty names and walked away. I can still recall his big moon-face, grinning at me over yellow teeth. The disturbing part about the whole incident was that a terrible feeling of guilt came over me as I realized that I had chosen the picture of the white girl over the
20   available pictures of black girls. I tried to rationalize it away,

but I was fascinated by the truth involved. Why hadn't I thought about it in this light before? So I took hold of the question and began to inquire into my feelings. Was it true, did I really prefer white girls over black? The conclusion was clear and inescapable: I did. I decided to check out my friends on this point and it was easy to determine, from listening to their general conversation, that the white woman occupied a peculiarly prominent place in all of our frames of reference. With what I have learned since then, this all seems
30 terribly elementary now. But at the time, it was a tremendously intriguing adventure of discovery.

One afternoon, when a large group of Negroes[1] was on the prison yard shooting the breeze, I grabbed the floor and posed the question: which did they prefer, white women or
35 black? Some said Japanese women were their favourite, others said Chinese, some said European women, others said Mexican women — they all stated a preference, and they generally freely admitted their dislike for black women.

'I don't want nothing black but a Cadillac,'[2] said one.
40 'If money was black I wouldn't want none of it,' put in another. (pp. 20-21)

Eldridge Cleaver
in the late 1970's

Questions:

1. Why wouldn't the prison guard let Cleaver have a girl pin-up on his cell wall?
2. Why did Cleaver feel so guilty?
3. Why did some black prisoners say they wanted nothing to do with anything black?

Words:

Enforced (line 9) – put into effect
Compromise (line 11) – make a deal
Rationalize (line 20) – try to give a logical or reasonable explanation
Prominent (line 28) – outstanding
Intriguing (line 31) – puzzling but fascinating

Notes:

1. *Negroes* This used to be the most popular way of describing people of the black race who have their origins in Africa. The word fell out of favour with black people during the late

35

1960's, because it seemed to avoid the proud use of the word black to describe black people.

2. *Cadillac* A big, flashy, expensive American car.

Selection 2

In the Southern States of America, a black man who flirted with a white woman had to suffer a heavy penalty.

My interest in this area persisted undiminished and then, in 1955, an event took place in Mississippi[1] which turned me inside out: Emmett Till, a young Negro down from Chicago[2] on a visit, was murdered, allegedly for flirting with a white
5   woman. He had been shot, his head crushed from repeated blows with a blunt instrument, and his badly decomposed body was recovered from the river with a heavy weight on it. I was, of course, angry over the whole bit, but one day I saw in a magazine a picture of the white woman with whom
10 Emmett Till was said to have flirted. While looking at the picture, I felt that little tension in the centre of my chest I experience when a woman appeals to me. I was disgusted and angry with myself. Here was a woman who had caused the death of a black, possibly because, when he looked at her, he
15 also felt the same tensions of lust and desire in his chest — and probably for the same reasons that I felt them. It was all unacceptable to me. I looked at the picture again and again, and in spite of everything and against my will and the hate I felt for the woman and all that she represented, she
20 appealed to me. I flew into a rage at myself, at America, white women, at the history that had placed those tensions of lust and desire in my chest. (p.23)

Questions:

1. Why was Emmett Till murdered?
2. How did Cleaver feel when he saw the picture of the white woman in the magazine?
3. Why was Cleaver so angry with himself?

Words:

Undiminished (line 1) – not getting less, not growing smaller

Allegedly (line 4) – supposedly
Decomposed (line 6) – rotted, decayed

Notes:
1. *Mississippi* One of the States in the south of the U.S.A. Well known for its brutal treatment of black people.
2. *Chicago* One of the leading cities in the northern state of Illinois.

Selection 3

Malcolm X had once claimed that black people were special. Here he states that what a man says and does is more important than his skin colour

'You may be shocked by these words coming from me, but I have always been a man who tries to face facts and to accept the reality of life as new experiences and knowledge unfold it. The experiences of this pilgrimage have taught me
5   much and each hour in the Holy Land[1] opens my eyes even more . . . I have eaten from the same plate with people whose eyes were the bluest of blue, whose hair was the blondest of blond and whose skin was the whitest of white . . . and

Malcolm X

I felt the sincerity in the words and deeds of these "white"
10   Muslims[2] that I felt among the African Muslims of Nigeria,
Sudan, and Ghana.'

Many of us were shocked and outraged by these words
from Malcolm X,[3] who had been a major influence upon us
all and the main factor in many of our conversions to the
15   Black Muslims.[4] But there were those of us who were glad
to be liberated from a doctrine of hate and racial supremacy.
The onus of teaching racial supremacy and hate, which is
the white man's burden, is pretty hard to bear. Asked if he
would accept whites as members of his Organization of Afro-
20   American Unity, Malcolm said he would accept John Brown[5]
if he were around today — which certainly is setting the
standard high.   (p.61)

Questions:

1. The first paragraph shows Malcolm X's joy at being able to
work well with people of different colours and races. Why do
you think that people of different colours find it so hard to
work together and mix together?
2. The word Afro-American has meaning because most of the
black people in America have ancestors who came from
Africa. Why have so many black people ended up in America?

Words:

Pilgrimage (line 4) — journey to a holy place or to a place which
is greatly respected or admired
Supremacy (line 16) — superiority

Notes:

1. *Holy Land* Another name for Palestine.
2. *Muslims* Followers of a religion based on the worship of Allah
(God) whose prophet is Mohammed and his teachings are
contained in a holy book called the Koran.
3. *Malcolm X* An extremely important black figure. His name
was Malcolm Little and he was born in Omaha in 1925. He
grew up in the state of Michigan. After leaving home and
school at a young age, he moved to Harlem, New York, and
became involved in thieving, pimping and drug-selling. When
he was 19, he was jailed for ten years. While in prison he
educated himself and became a strong believer in the Black

Muslim religion which among other things preached that blacks were superior to whites, and called for the separation of the black and white races. Later in 1963 he changed his mind on these points and so was forced to leave the Black Muslims. After travelling to African and Arab countries, he started the Organization of Afro-American Unity. He now believed that some blacks and whites could work together, but that blacks needed to build their own independent organizations to develop self-respect and pride, and to decide on their own path to achieve freedom. In his autobiography, which Alex Haley, the author of *Roots*, helped him to write, he made it clear that he expected to be killed by Black Muslims. In 1965 he was shot dead at a meeting by men believed to be Black Muslim supporters.

4. *Black Muslims* A black religious group which became popular during the 1950's. It built up black pride in an age when blacks suffered humiliation from white racists, by stating that black and white races should be separated. In recent years the Black Muslims have grown into a big business organization. The boxer Muhammed Ali belonged to the Black Muslims until he was expelled in 1969. Black Muslims refuse to vote or do military service in the U.S.A. They also forbid smoking and drinking, and insist that women should be dominated by men.

5. *John Brown* A white American, born in 1800, who took up arms to try to help black slaves to gain their freedom. He was caught and hanged for his activities in 1859.

Some young white people have realized that many of the biggest heroes in white history and culture have a terrible record of violence, greed, cruelty and selfishness.

What has suddenly happened is that the white race has lost its heroes. Worse, its heroes have been revealed as villains and its greatest heroes as the arch-villains. The new genera-tions of whites, appalled by the sanguine and despicable
5 record carved over the face of the globe by their race in the last five hundred years, are rejecting the panoply of white heroes, whose heroism consisted in erecting the inglorious edifice of colonialism and imperialism; heroes whose careers rested on a system of foreign and domestic exploitation,
10 rooted in the myth of white supremacy and the manifest destiny of the white race. The emerging shape of a new world order, and the requisites for survival in such a world, are fostering in young whites a new outlook. They recoil in shame from the spectacle of cowboys and pioneers — their heroic
15 forefathers whose exploits filled earlier generations with pride — galloping across a movie screen shooting down Indians like Coke bottles. Even Winston Churchill,[1] who is looked upon by older whites as perhaps the greatest hero of the twentieth century — even he, because of the system of
20 which he was a creature and which he served, is an arch-villain in the eyes of the young white rebels.   (pp. 71-72)

Questions:
1. Why does Cleaver think that the white race has lost its heroes?
2. Have you ever felt angry when watching cowboys in a film "shooting down Indians like Coke bottles"? If you have felt angry say why.

Words:
Appalled (line 4) – shocked, horrified
Sanguine (line 4) – bloody
Despicable (line 4) – disgraceful
Inglorious (line 7) – shameful
Edifice (line 8) – structure, framework
Colonialism (line 8) – system in which one country takes over

another to exploit it, and has complete control over it

Imperialism (line 8) – system like colonialism. One country controls another without taking it over completely, but by dominating its economy, way of thinking and way of life. The economy is dominated through multi-national companies. The way of thinking and way of life are dominated by books, magazines, films, music, TV, radio, etc.

Supremacy (line 10) – superiority or controlling influence over

Myth (line 10) – false idea believed by many people

Requisites (line 12) necessary things, things needed

Notes:

1. *Winston Churchill* Famous British politician, born in 1874 and died in 1965. Had an extremely long political career. Became a Conservative M.P. in 1900. Was Prime Minister of the British Government during the 2nd World War 1940-45, and was Conservative Prime Minister 1951-1955. He did not believe that black people should have freedom. He believed strongly that the British should have the right to rule over black African countries as well as over Asian countries like India.

Vietnamese victory over the Americans in Vietnam

Selection 5

A lot of white people are beginning to learn the truth about their history.

The rebellion of the oppressed peoples of the world, along with the Negro revolution in America, have opened the way to a new evaluation of history, a re-examination of the role played by the white race since the beginning of European
5 expansion. The positive achievements are also there in the record, and future generations will applaud them. But there can be no applause now, not while the master still holds the whip in his hand! Not even the master's own children can find it possible to applaud him — he cannot even applaud
10 himself! The negative rings too loudly. Slave-catchers, slave-owners, murderers, butchers, invaders, oppressors — the white heroes have acquired new names. The great white statesmen whom school children are taught to revere are revealed as the architects of systems of human exploitation
15 and slavery. Religious leaders are exposed as condoners and justifiers of all these evil deeds. Schoolteachers and college professors are seen as a clique of brainwashers and white-washers.

The white youth of today are coming to see, intuitively,
20 that to escape the onus of the history their fathers made they must face and admit the moral truth concerning the works of their fathers. That such venerated figures as George

Washington[1] and Thomas Jefferson[2] owned hundreds of black slaves, that all of the Presidents up to Lincoln[3] presided
25 over a slave state, and that every President since Lincoln connived politically and cynically with the issues affecting the human rights and general welfare of the broad masses of the American people — these facts weigh heavily upon the hearts of these young people.   (pp. 72-73)

Questions:
1. Why does Cleaver think that many white heroes in history should be given new names?
2. Why does Cleaver have no respect for George Washington who was the first President of the U.S.A.?

Words:
Oppressed (line 1) – unjustly treated, cruelly treated

Evaluation (line 3) – judgement

Acquired (line 12) – got, gained

Revere (line 13) – respect, admire

Exploitation (line 14) – making unfair use of people, selfish use of other people

Condoners (line 15) – forgivers, excusers

Clique (line 17) – small exclusive group of people with the same views

Intuitively (line 19) – without thinking deeply

Onus (line 20) – responsibility, burden

Venerated (line 22) – highly respected

Frelimo freedom fighter in Mozambique

Notes:
1. *George Washington* Born 1732, died 1799. Was a strong supporter of the American independence struggle against Britain. Afterwards he became the first President of the U.S.A. He was also a big slave-owner.
2. *Thomas Jefferson* Born 1743, died 1826. President of the U.S.A. from 1801 to 1809. Like George Washington, he talked a lot about human rights while at the same time being a big slave-owner.
3. *Abraham Lincoln* Born 1809 in the state of Kentucky. Became President of the U.S.A. in 1860 and was in office during the American Civil War, and at the time when the slaves were officially freed in 1863. Was murdered by shooting in 1865.

Most whites in America have never worried about the murder of blacks. So blacks gained some protection when whites joined their demonstrations.

The third stage, which is rapidly drawing to a close, emerged when white youth started joining Negro demonstrations in large numbers. The presence of whites among the demonstrators emboldened the Negro leaders and allowed them to
5   use tactics they never would have been able to employ with all-black troops. The racist conscience of America is such that murder does not register as murder, really, unless the victim is white. And it was only when the newspapers and magazines started carrying pictures and stories of white demonstrators
10   being beaten and maimed by mobs and police that the public began to protest. Negroes have become so used to this double standard that they, too, react differently to the death of a white. When white freedom riders were brutalized along with blacks, a sigh of relief went up from the black masses,
15   because the blacks knew that white blood is the coin of freedom in a land where for four hundred years black blood has been shed unremarked and with impunity. America has never truly been outraged by the murder of a black man, woman, or child. White politicians may, if Negroes are
20   aroused by a particular murder, say with their lips what they know with their minds they should feel with their hearts — but don't.   (p 75)

Questions:
1. Why did black people find it useful when white people joined in their protest demonstrations?
2. Do you think it is true that white people and black people don't take the death of a black person as seriously as that of a white person? Try to give some examples.

Words:
Emboldened (line 4) – gave courage to
Maimed (line 10) – crippled
Impunity (line 17) – freedom from punishment

White youths in America join black demonstrations

As situations change, whites develop new reasons and methods for keeping black people down.

Let us recall that the white man, in order to justify slavery and, later on, to justify segregation, elaborated a complex, all-pervasive myth which at one time classified the black man as a subhuman beast of burden. The myth was progressively
5 modified, gradually elevating the blacks on the scale of evolution, following their slowly changing status, until the plateau of separate-but-equal was reached at the close of the nineteenth century. During slavery, the black was seen as a mindless Supermasculine Menial. Forced to do the back-
10 breaking work, he was conceived in terms of his ability to do such work — 'field niggers', etc. The white man administered the plantation, doing all the thinking, exercising omnipotent power over the slaves. He had little difficulty dissociating himself from the black slaves, and he could not conceive of
15 their positions being reversed or even reversible.

(pp. 79-80)

Questions:

1. Does the white man still expect the black man to stick to hard, back-breaking work? Give some examples.
2. Why did the white man try to say that the black man was subhuman?

Words:

Segregation (line 2) – the separation of people of different races
Myth (line 3) – false idea believed by many people
Evolution (line 6) – the gradual development of the human race to higher levels of civilization
Plateau (line 7) – steady situation
Menial (line 9) – person doing humiliating work, low-level servant
Omnipotent (line 12) – unlimited power

*Young whites have a chance to earn respect from black people,
but only if they reject the evil actions of their fathers and grand-
fathers.*

From the beginning of the contact between blacks and
whites, there has been very little reason for a black man to
respect a white, with such exceptions as John Brown and
others lesser known. But respect commands itself and it can
5 neither be given nor withheld when it is due. If a man like
Malcolm X could change and repudiate racism, if I myself
and other former Muslims can change, if young whites can
change, then there is hope for America. It was certainly
strange to find myself, while steeped in the doctrine that all
10 whites were devils by nature, commanded by the heart to
applaud and acknowledge respect for these young whites —
despite the fact that they are descendants of the masters
and I the descendant of slave. The sins of the fathers are
visited upon the heads of the children — but only if the
15 children continue in the evil deeds of the fathers.

(pp. 83-84)

Questions:
1. What does racism mean?
2. The Black Muslims in America think that all whites are devils
   by nature. What do you think of this?

Words:
Repudiate (line 6) – refuse to accept
Doctrine (line 9) – teaching, belief
Descendants (line 12) – children

Selection 9

*Whites are clever at getting famous blacks to work against the
interests of their own people. Famous blacks who speak out for
their own people face serious problems.*

Paul Robeson[1] was at the apex of an illustrious career as a
singer and actor, earning over $200,000 a year, when he
began speaking out passionately on behalf of his people,

unable to balance the luxury of his own life with the squalor
5 of the black masses from which he sprang and of which he
was proud. The response of the black masses to his charisma
alarmed both the Uncle Toms and the white power structure,
and Paul Robeson was marked for destruction. Through a
co-ordinated, sustained effort, Robeson became the object of
10 economic boycott and character assassination. Broken
financially, and heartbroken to see black Uncle Toms working
assiduously to defeat him and keep their own people down,
Robeson's spirit was crushed, his health subverted, and his
career destroyed.
15 By crushing black leaders, while inflating the images of
Uncle Toms and celebrities from the apolitical world of
sport and play, the mass media were able to channel and control the aspirations and goals of the black masses. The effect
was to take the 'problem' out of a political and economic and
20 philosophical context and place it on the misty level of
'goodwill', 'charitable and harmonious race relations', and
'good sportsmanlike conduct'. This technique of 'Negro
control' has been so effective that the best-known Negroes in
America have always been — and still are — the entertainers

Paul Robeson

25   and athletes (this is true also of white America). The
tradition is that whenever a crisis with racial overtones arises,
an entertainer or athlete is trotted out and allowed to expound a predictable, conciliatory interpretation of what's
happening. The mass media rush forward with grinding
30   cameras and extended microphones as though some great
oracle were about to lay down a new covenant from God;
when in reality, all that has happened is that the blacks have
been sold out and cooled out again — 'One more time,
boom! One more time, boom!'   (pp. 88-89)

Questions:

1. What are black Uncle Toms?
2. Why are the best known negroes in America entertainers and athletes?
3. Why did so many people treat Paul Robeson badly?

Words:

Illustrious (line 1) – famous, distinguished

Charisma (line 6) – a personality which other people find highly attractive

Character assassination (line 10) – dishonest attempt to destroy his reputation

Assiduously (line 12) – constantly

Expound (line 27) – explain, put forward

Conciliatory (line 28) – peaceful, friendly

Mass media (line 29) – television, radio, newspapers which reach a large number of people

Oracle (line 31) – person in direct contact with God

Notes:

1. *Paul Robeson* Paul Robeson was a black American born in Princeton, New Jersey in 1898. He was one of the greatest singers the world has ever seen. His father was born a slave but fought his way to freedom becoming first a teacher and later a preacher. In his youth Robeson and other blacks had to face racial prejudice, which was widespread in the U.S. and which denied blacks a good education or well-paid jobs. Nevertheless, he won a scholarship, in 1915, to an exclusive white university called Rutgers College.

    He became an American football superstar. However, at

first, white students at Rutgers College had not wanted a black man in their team so they had broken Robeson's nose and hand. They also dislocated his shoulder. Paul Robeson graduated from Rutgers with the highest academic honours, then went on to qualify as a lawyer. Next, he became famous as an actor and singer. He lived in Britain from 1927 to 1929. While in London, Robeson not only developed his acting and singing career but also studied the language, history and music of Africa. Although he was an American he strongly identified with black people in Africa. In his film and stage acting as well as in his singing, Paul Robeson tried his best to play roles which gave the black man self-respect. When World War 2 started in 1939, Robeson returned to the U.S.A. and stayed there until the war ended in 1945. After the war, the American government turned against Robeson because he defended the Soviet Union and refused to attack the Russians or Communism. He had visited the Soviet Union in 1934 and had discovered that the Russians treated black people with more respect than he had ever experienced in his home country of America. From 1947 to 1949, Robeson put his career second so that he could spend more time fighting for black people's rights in the U.S. In 1950 the U.S. government took away Paul Robeson's passport, so that from 1950 to 1958 he was not able to travel to follow his job as an actor and singer. They also saw to it that inside America itself, theatres, concert halls, radio, TV, and recording studios were closed to him. Even when he published a book called *Here I Stand* in 1958, white newspapers and magazines refused to mention it. Despite this, white people in Britain helped him by arranging for him to sing for British people over the telephone from the U.S. Two concerts were arranged for him in this way in 1957. The first one had an audience of 1000 people in St. Pancras Town Hall, London. The second was arranged by South Wales miners and had an audience of 5000 Welsh people. In 1958 after he got back his passport, he went to London and sang in St. Paul's Cathedral. 4000 people were inside the Church with another 5000 standing outside.

In 1961, Paul Robeson became ill. He returned to the U.S. and retired in 1963.

He died in 1976.

Selection 10

White America would only tolerate black boxing champions who used their fists in the ring and kept their mouths shut outside it. Until Muhammad Ali became champion, most black boxers were scared to use their brains outside the boxing ring to maintain their self-respect.

There is no doubt that white America will accept a black champion, applaud and reward him, as long as there is no 'white hope' in sight. But what white America demands in her black champions is a brilliant, powerful body and a dull
5 bestial mind — a tiger in the ring and a pussycat outside the ring. It is a hollow, cruel mockery to crown a man king in the boxing ring and then shove him about outside, going so far as to burn a cross on his front doorstep, as whites did when Floyd Patterson[1] tried to integrate a neighbourhood.
10 'A man's home is his castle' is a saying not meant for Negroes; a Negro's castle exists only in his mind. And for a black king of boxing the boundaries of his kingdom are sharply circumscribed by the ropes around the ring. A slave in private life, a king in public — this is the life that every
15 black champion has had to lead — until the coming of Muhammad Ali.

Muhammad Ali is the first 'free' black champion ever to confront white America. (p. 91)

Muhammed Ali one of the greatest boxers of all time

Questions:

1. Why do white Americans want black boxing champions to have brilliant bodies and dull minds?
2. What should a black person do if he becomes rich and famous? Should he:
   a. Behave in a way that will please white people and make them think better of blacks; or
   b. Behave in a way that will please black people but make white people angry and scared?
3. What would you do to help other black people if you became rich and famous?

Words:

Bestial (line 5) – like an animal or beast.
Circumscribed (line 13) – limited.

51

Notes:

1. *Floyd Patterson* Black American boxer. Born in North Carolina in 1935. He became World Heavyweight boxing champion in 1956. He lost the title in 1959, got it back in 1960, then lost it again in 1962. He fought Muhammad Ali for the title in 1965. Ali thrashed him. Before the fight Ali claimed that whites wanted to see Patterson win because they felt that Patterson was a "tame black man" while Ali was an "uppity nigger" (i.e. a black man who needed to be put in his place).

   Patterson's last fight was in 1972, when he fought Ali again. Ali stopped him in the seventh round.

Selection 11

Norman Podhoretz, a white journalist, describes the jealousy he feels at the way black people move.

'. . . just as in childhood I envied Negroes for what seemed to me their superior masculinity, so I envy them today for what seems to me their superior physical grace and beauty. I have come to value physical grace very highly, and I am
5 now capable of aching with all my being when I watch a Negro couple on the dance floor, or a Negro playing baseball or basketball. *They are on the kind of terms with their own bodies that I should like to be on with mine, and for that precious quality they seem blessed to me.*' Norman Pod-
10 horetz: 'My Negro Problem — and Ours', *Commentary*, February, 1963.   (p. 173)

Questions:

1. Why is it that often white people are jealous of black people?
2. What quality does the writer feel that black people have which he does not have?

Words:

Masculinity (line 2) – male features
Physical (line 3) – to do with the body
Grace (line 3) – elegance